How To Manage Money

A Comprehensive Handbook For Adolescents Detailing Strategies For Financial Management, Proficient Communication, And Goal Attainment

(Assert Dominance Over Your Finances Through The Establishment Of Financial Objectives)

Eberhard Gutmann

TABLE OF CONTENT

Life Insurance

This particular one does not offer any advantages or benefits to you. You do not derive any benefits/profits/gains from it. Nevertheless, it provides reassurance for the financial well-being of your family in the event of an unfortunate incident. Despite the challenges associated with broaching this subject within the family sphere, it remains a vital undertaking that significantly impacts the well-being of your loved ones.

In addition to your affection, your family is dependent on you to provide financial stability. Particularly if you are the only source of income.

In the course of instructing individuals on matters of personal finance, I have encountered numerous households wherein the sole provider tragically and unexpectedly passed away prior to their offspring attaining educational completion.

In each of these instances, a consistent level of melancholy has been observed. There are no viable measures that can be taken to alleviate the psychological anguish experienced by the family.

However, there exists a significant disparity in their levels of gratitude.

It may be arduous to conceive at present, but the matter of financial loss is not one that can be regarded with levity.

Acquiring term life insurance is a prudent investment.

If you are in receipt of income and you are responsible for supporting individuals who rely on you,

Should you possess any outstanding financial liabilities,

If you hold the belief that your dependents or family members would be unable to sustain their current standard of living in the event of a loss of income.

The primary dilemma arises in selecting the most suitable life insurance scheme. Your uncle proffers a proposition, while your friends propose an alternative. Web Aggregators provide users with a comprehensive compilation that is difficult to comprehend or decipher.

The response, however, becomes significantly straightforward once one acquires knowledge, commits it to memory, and consistently recites a singular truth.

Insurance should not be regarded as an investment.

Insurance does not serve as a suitable instrument for tax mitigation.

Insurance is an expense. Hence, it is imperative that we handle it in a similar manner. Most importantly, it should be noted that the purpose of insurance is to mitigate risk. Nothing more, nothing less. The purpose of insuring your vehicle is not to generate profits. Conversely, you are providing an additional fee in order to mitigate the likelihood of a potentially higher payment in the future.

It is not advisable to opt for a non-term plan or any investment vehicle that provides minimal or no returns. The premiums associated with these plans are excessively elevated. The returns are excessively low, as is the level of coverage (the sum of money provided to the family in the event of death).

Allocating this sum of money to an alternative investment option would result in significantly greater financial gains. Regrettably, the fundamental objective of life insurance, namely to offer sufficient coverage, remains unmet.

In the event of term insurance, no return is received unless the stipulations of the insurance policy are enacted. That is to say, at the moment of the individual's demise as covered by the insurance policy. This measure is taken with the purpose of guaranteeing that your family remains financially secure even in the most dire circumstances.

Taking into consideration the impact of inflation, the life insurance payout is projected to adequately provide for your family's needs for a period spanning approximately 6 to 8 years. This will provide them with a sufficient duration to devise alternative means of generating revenue.

To provide greater precision, the sum should encompass your family's ongoing cost of living, significant expenditures, and any outstanding debt.

The current required value for your Term Insurance claim may be considerably lesser than the amount that will be necessary after a span of 30 years. Always account for inflation.

Therefore, it is advisable to select a policy that gradually enhances your coverage to a minimum of twice the original amount by the conclusion of the term.

It is not permissible to 'upgrade' your Term Insurance policy. Exercise caution when selecting one.

Please ensure that your cover is sufficient.

In most instances, it is advisable to secure insurance coverage until the age at which you intend to retire, typically 60 years old. This milestone likewise marks the period in which family members achieve autonomy. It is advised to refrain from succumbing to the allure of whole-life insurance policies. The insurance premiums experience a significant increase, while the returns demonstrate a lackluster performance.

Consider add-on factors like:

Insurance coverage for accidents, which entails a predetermined payout based on the nature and severity of the injuries sustained. Please take it into consideration solely if you have a propensity for frequent travel. Furthermore, it disburses an additional monetary amount to the designated beneficiary in the event of the policyholder's demise resulting from an accident.

Future Premium Waiver is a provision wherein, in the event of an accident or fulfillment of certain predetermined conditions, your premium payments will cease, while the policy remains in effect.

For critical illness benefit, accidental death benefit, and accidental disability; consider taking policies particularly for these instead of taking them as riders.

To conclude the selection of the company from which to secure life insurance:

opt for a reputable brand,

possessing a favorable claim settlement ratio (the quotient obtained by dividing the number of claims they fulfill by the total number of claims received), satisfactory settlement ratio (the ratio of the amount paid for these claims to the total amount claimed) Certain companies have gained notoriety for settling small claims while delaying the resolution of larger ones. This enables them to maintain their claim settlement ratio while simultaneously posing challenges for larger claims.

Favorable solvency ratio (all efforts will be in vain if the company lacks sufficient funds to meet critical financial obligations during periods of utmost importance to your family).

An additional significant provision that the company should offer is a functionality known as income benefit. In the event that you choose this option, as opposed to receiving a one-time payment, your family will receive a predetermined income for a specified duration. This is something that facilitates individuals in swiftly regaining stability.

I have consistently advocated against the disbursement of complete sums to any individual. There exist a multitude of instances wherein individuals have attained wealth through winning lotteries, receiving inheritances, and similar circumstances. Engaging in fraudulent tactics to reclaim the sums acquired and expeditiously restore their former financial positions. By choosing this alternative, you have the opportunity to reduce your premium.

An alternative course of action would be to implement a progressive increment in monthly disbursements, wherein the disbursement amount would be augmented annually in order to accommodate rising expenses arising from inflation.

An alternative option is to select the monthly income lump-sum alternative, in which a portion of the payout is provided upfront, with the remaining amount being disbursed on a monthly basis.

Naturally, not every company provides each and every option available.

◆◆◆

What exclusions are typically specified in a conventional Term Insurance policy?

This varies depending on the specific policy, but a majority of companies have provisions that exclude coverage for death resulting from acts of terrorism, armed conflicts, and calamities of a natural origin. This is due to the presence of a large number of claimants in these unfortunate circumstances.

In addition to these, fatalities resulting from suicide will not be eligible for coverage within a one-year time period. Compensation may not be awarded in cases where death is incurred during the commission of a criminal act.

A few additional tips:

The annual premium installments will be more cost-effective compared to the monthly payment option.

Do not conceal any instances of smoking or alcohol consumption from the insurance provider. While there is a possibility of a premium increase, failing to disclose relevant information would provide grounds for the company to challenge the claim.

Establish notifications for your premium payments.

Find out if the premium will remain constant throughout the policy, or if it will increase with time. It should remain constant.

Regrettably, the initial priority regarding the claim amount is allocated to your creditors; individuals or institutions from whom you have acquired loans. You have the option to pursue a clause that invokes the Married Women's Property Act. This will vest absolute entitlement to the proceeds of the policy in your wife and children.

Upon receiving your policy documents, it is imperative to thoroughly verify the particulars such as personal information, including your name, address, coverage details, among others.

It is advisable to contemplate acquiring loan insurance for any substantial loans one undertakes. In this manner, the premium will cease upon full repayment of the loan, and there is the potential to decrease the level of coverage provided by your term insurance policy, consequently reducing the associated premium payments.

The funds can be utilized for

funeral expenses,

to clear debts,

to assist in forthcoming expenditures, including routine household expenses as well as financial obligations such as children's education and matrimony.

In the absence of any other considerations, it can serve as a valuable financial inheritance for your family.

A notable benefit of Term Plans resides in the provision of substantial coverage at a nominal premium cost.

Who is it for?

It is imperative that individuals with financial dependents and insufficient accumulated wealth for future financial obligations should consider procuring a term insurance policy. This will ensure the provision of necessary funds to cater to the present and prospective financial requirements of their dependents.

Costs associated with the pursuit of advanced academia for dependents and marital partner

A home loan

Ambitious aspirations and festive festivities

Who is exempted from the need to make a purchase?

Not every individual necessitates the acquisition of a term insurance policy. There is no necessity for you to partake in one if -

You currently do not have any individuals who are financially dependent on you, and you do not anticipate having any in the near future.

You possess an ample amount of financial assets that will adequately support the monetary requirements of your family.

The sole condition is that in the event of surpassing the policy term, there is no reimbursement provided.

However, it offers your family an opportunity to regain stability and achieve financial success.

Term insurance provides beneficiaries with the precise amount of coverage as stated in the policy. In the event that your sum assured amount totals Rs2 crore, your designated beneficiary will be entitled to receive this sum. There are no fees or deductions applied to this. It is imperative that you guarantee the payment of your premiums throughout the duration of the policy.

Please remember to avail the deduction under Section 80C when filing your Income Tax Return.

Term insurance coverage needed: (1) (2) (3)

(1) Pension fund. In general, the customary approach is to have 25 times your yearly expenditures.

(2) Sufficient funds to settle all outstanding loans.

(3) Sufficient funds to fulfill all significant future financial objectives.

How can one ascertain the profitability of an insurance policy?

It is quite effortless to demonstrate significant figures when dealing with insurance policies that have lock-in periods of 25 years or more. "Each time you experience enthusiasm regarding the investment yields of a non-term policy offered by any insurance provider,

1) Determine the financial gains that would result from investing in a fixed deposit or recurring deposit with a nominal interest rate of 6.5%, as an alternative to making premium payments.

2) Inquire with the advisor regarding the guarantee of the bonus and F.A.B.

Engaging in this activity will provide you with a better comprehension as to why exclusive emphasis is placed on Term Insurance Plans.

You procure life insurance not solely due to the prospect of your mortality, but rather to ensure your family's ability to endure beyond your lifetime.

They will express their gratitude in the future.

If more than 75% of your total assets are comprised of your residence, it is strongly advised to give careful consideration to acquiring home insurance.

The Indian courts have witnessed numerous legal disputes that could have been preventable if there had been proper drafting, execution, and attestation of Wills, as well as seeking the guidance of professionals.

Professionals recommend recording the act of executing a Last Will and Testament in the presence of a medical professional, as well as obtaining a medical certificate to verify the mental competence of the person making the Will at the time of its execution.

Facilitate financial ease for your family.

Prerequisites Of Balance Sheet In Private Equity And Debt Financing

When an individual is making an investment in your company or providing financial backing, they request the submission of the balance sheet and financial statements. The examination and evaluation of financial statements holds significant importance for financiers as it enables them to make informed credit decisions. This tool is indispensable. A banking institution will grant credit unless the balance sheet and financial statement indicate that the company possesses...

a) Demonstrating solid financial stability (Solvency Assessment)

b) Adequate liquidity (cash flows)

c) Strong financial viability (profitability)

Typically, financial institutions have an expectation that the size of the firm's balance sheet should increase annually. The generated income from the business activities will be incorporated into the business's capital reserves. Profit can also derive from investment activities. There is a possibility of augmenting the machinery, thereby enhancing production and fostering an increase in sales. When it reaches a state of obsolescence, it is substituted with a newer alternative. When a company incurs losses, it will reduce its capital reserves. As a result of diminished sales revenue, amplified occurrence of uncollectible debts, subpar collection efforts, or depleted inventory levels due to inadequate liquidity to procure and adequately stock the merchandise. All of these factors will have an impact on the overall financial statement. Gaining comprehensive insight into the modifications, conducting a thorough assessment of their ramifications, and assessing their potential influence are indispensable for investors and financiers.

Categorization of Assets and Liabilities

For the purpose of analysis, assets and liabilities are categorized in a manner that facilitates ease and practicality.

1) Investments 2) Equity 3) Property 4) Holdings 5) Resources

Assets are categorically classified into

a) Tangible Assets

b) Assets held by the entity that are expected to be converted into cash, sold, or consumed within one year or the normal operating cycle, whichever is longer.

c) Long-term Assets

"d) Non-physical Assets

2) Obligations or debt

a)Capital and Reserves

b) Current liabilities

c) Liabilities with mid-range and extended durations

Assets

"a) Tangible Assets

Fixed Assets, also referred to as Block assets, are tangible capital assets that hold value for a business. These include durable assets with long periods of usefulness, such as land, buildings, plants and machinery, vehicles, furniture and fixtures, tools, and dies.

b) Current Assets

Capital assets are considered a form of highly liquid assets. These items are retained with the intention of selling or converting them into cash within a span of 12 months. Current assets consist of Cash, Cash equivalents, Sundry Debtors, inventory of stock, marketable securities, prepaid liabilities, and other liquid assets. Current assets play a crucial role in the business as they facilitate daily operational activities and enable timely settlement of ongoing operating expenses.

c) Non-Current Assets

Non-current assets refer to assets that are not anticipated to be converted into cash, utilized, or disposed of within a 12-month period from the date specified on the balance sheet, excluding fixed assets. This encompasses investments made in subsidiary companies, affiliated entities within the same corporate group, unquoted investments, outstanding book debts exceeding a duration of 180 days, advancements made to suppliers of capital goods, and non-consumable stores and spare parts.

d) Non-physical assets / Intangible assets

These are not physical. Goodwill, Brands, and intellectual property, such as patents, trademarks, and copyrights, are examples of intangible assets.

Fictitious assets are inherently intangible and lack a tangible existence. They can be categorized as deferred revenue expenditures, from which the advantages are derived over an extended duration.

Instances of spurious assets include 1. Advertising expenditures of an enterprise.

2. Preliminary expenses 3. A reduction in the price of shares issued, amounting to 4%. The financial detriment arising from the issuance of debentures.

All assets categorized as fictitious are intangibles, however, not all intangible assets fall under the classification of fictitious assets.

Liabilities

a) Capital and Retained Earnings.

Capital refers to the financial resources that are contributed by proprietors or stakeholders towards the establishment and operation of a business. The profits obtained from the business are accumulated and included herein. Reserves are generated from earnings that are specifically designated for this purpose. A portion of the reserves comprises Revenue and Capital reserves.

b) Liabilities that are due within the current fiscal year

Present obligations that are due within a short period of time are categorized as current liabilities. All obligations that must be settled within a period of 12 months are classified within this particular category. Current liabilities are commonly employed for the purpose of discharging current assets, which typically expire within a span of 12 months. A few examples of the existing short-term obligations include accounts payable, unpaid bills, tax payables, and bank loan limits. Term loan installments that are set to mature within the upcoming 12 months are categorized within this category.

Optimal Strategies for Saving

We all aspire to achieve financial savings. Each individual possesses their unique approach to saving funds, be it through abstaining from a weekly indulgence in a $4 mocha latte or postponing a luxurious family getaway.

These prudent recommendations have the potential to assist you in devising optimal strategies to curb expenses in your daily existence.

1. Pay Off Your Debt.

If you are seeking to achieve financial savings through budgeting, it is advisable to prioritize addressing your debt situation if you currently have substantial outstanding obligations. Not persuaded? This can be easily ascertained by summing up the monthly amount allocated towards debt repayment. Once the obligation to pay interest on your debt ceases, you can readily allocate those funds towards one's savings. A viable alternative for debt consolidation, facilitating improved repayment, is the utilization of a personal line of credit.

2. Make savings objectives.

Envisioning the objective of your savings constitutes an exemplary strategy for frugality. Establishing savings targets and implementing a set timeframe can serve as motivational factors towards initiating a savings endeavor. Are you interested in making a down payment of 20% towards the acquisition of a residential property within a three-year timeframe? Now that you have established an objective, you are now aware of the financial amount that must be allocated on a monthly basis in order to accomplish it. Utilize the savings calculators offered by Regions to set and pursue your financial objectives.

3. Prioritize your own needs.

Establish a systematic transfer arrangement on a recurring basis, whereby funds are regularly transferred from your checking account to your savings account after each payday. Do not deprive yourself of a prudent and sustainable savings strategy, regardless of whether it entails setting aside $50 biweekly or $500.

4. Quit smoking.

No, ceasing smoking is not a straightforward endeavor. However, individuals who consume a pack and a half of cigarettes daily could potentially conserve nearly $3,000 annually by abstaining from this habit. Enroll in the association: according to the Centers for Disease Control, the proportion of the American population engaged in smoking has fallen below 20% for the first instance since at least the mid-1960s.

5. Go on a \\\"Staycation\\\".

The idea is well-founded: rather than investing significant amounts of money in costly overseas air travel, consider exploring local destinations near your residence for delightful vacations. If it is not feasible to embark on a long journey by car, we recommend exploring economical flight options within your vicinity.

6. Invest to Save.

Considering that utility expenses generally do not exhibit a tendency to decrease over time, it is prudent to weatherize your residence promptly, prior to a situation where it becomes impractical. Please contact your utility company and inquire about arranging an energy audit. Alternatively, seek assistance from a licensed professional who can evaluate the energy efficiency of your entire household. This can be achieved through a range of measures, including but not limited to basic modifications such as the proper sealing of windows and doors, as well as more substantial upgrades like the installment of improved insulation, siding, or ENERGY STAR certified high-efficiency appliances and products. Over the course of time, significant savings can be realized in terms of utility expenses.

7. Energy Savings.

By decreasing the water heater's thermostat by a margin of 10°F, you have the potential to reduce energy expenditure and achieve a cost saving of approximately 3-5 percent on your energy bills. Moreover, the implementation of an on-demand or tankless water heater has the potential to generate cost reductions of approximately 30% in comparison to a conventional storage tank water heater.

8. Bring lunch.

Discovering consistent savings represents a definitive strategy for prudent financial management. By refraining from purchasing lunch at work, which amounts to $7, and opting instead for a packed lunch from home, priced at $2, you have the potential to amass a substantial emergency fund of $1250 or substantially boost your dedication to a retirement or college savings scheme within a span of 12 months.

9. Open a Money-Giving Account.

For the majority of individuals, maintaining a division between one's savings and checking accounts aids in reducing the inclination to sporadically borrow from savings. For enhanced cost-effectiveness, particularly in cases of longer-term goals, we recommend exploring financial products with higher yield rates such as a Regions CD or a Regions Money Market account.

10. Make Your Expenses Annual.

Are you consistently allotting $20 per week for the purchase of snacks from the office vending machine? You are allocating $1,000 per annum from your financial budget for the purpose of purchasing carbonated beverages and refreshments. Such a habit unexpectedly results in a significant expense.

Chapter 4: The Concept and Advantages of Saving

Put simply, saving pertains to a portion of one's earnings that has not been expended. If the funds are not set aside, there is a likelihood of their utilization. The concept of saving entails the preservation of a sufficient amount of monetary resources for utilization during unforeseen circumstances. You do not simply set aside all of your funds; instead, you allocate a portion towards investment in order to generate growth and increase the total sum. What are the reasons or justifications for implementing saving practices in the first instance? Let's explore the advantages of practicing savings:

Having a sufficient financial reserve provides individuals with a sense of tranquility and emotional gratification, as it ensures that they are adequately prepared to handle unforeseen monetary obligations.

Disregard the use of piggy banks as an adequate method of managing your finances; the allocation of funds into a savings account will facilitate the multiplication of your wealth. The marginal returns derived from your savings will prove to be substantial in the long run.

The capacity to accumulate savings imparts upon you the attribute of fiscal prudence, a skill that shall undoubtedly prove advantageous in the foreseeable future.

By actively saving, you can effectively avoid accumulating debt and secure a smoother path towards achieving your financial objectives.

There will inevitably be a point in your existence when your level of physical activity and capacity for employment will diminish. Making savings will enable you to take care of your future self by utilizing the earnings you are currently striving for.

Accruing savings will allow you to amass a substantial sum towards a significant aspiration, such as securing a down payment for a residence. It will aid in alleviating the burden of monthly payments and securing more favorable interest rates.

Accumulating savings can subsequently provide significant utility when financing your own education or that of your offspring.

By means of diligent saving, one can embark on a highly anticipated vacation that may otherwise remain unattainable unless a predetermined sum is accumulated over a certain duration.

If you assume the role of a financially responsible parent or older sibling, you actively cultivate a savings-oriented mindset that will undeniably benefit your children or younger siblings.

There exist substantial advantages, varying in magnitude, pertaining to the act of saving. However, the overarching principle at play is that saving grants individuals a sense of financial autonomy that might otherwise remain unattainable. Despite being aware of the multitude of advantages associated with saving, a significant portion of individuals fail to engage in this financial practice. What are the contributing factors that render this task particularly challenging?

The Challenge of Saving: Understanding the Difficulty

The primary reason why many individuals are unable to save is not due to lack of desire or lack of financial resources, but rather their aspiration to accumulate substantial savings within a specific timeframe. Due to the potential unavailability of substantial sums, many individuals reconcile themselves to not engaging in savings.

The Truth

Accumulating savings does not depend on substantial sums, but rather on setting aside a portion of one's income or resources. Setting aside $5 each month constitutes a deliberate act of saving and embarking on a modest beginning serves as the sole method of self-instruction in the discipline of saving.

Please take note that unforeseen circumstances in life can disrupt your meticulously devised financial plan, but by implementing a structured savings strategy, you can withstand such challenges with relative ease.

There is truly no more opportune moment to commence the act of saving than the present time. Do not procrastinate until securing a more financially lucrative occupation or until your spouse procures employment. It is imperative to maintain a lifestyle that is within your means by limiting expenses to an amount lower than your income, subsequently setting aside any remaining funds, regardless of the magnitude, for savings.

In order to facilitate the process of achieving comprehensive financial management, the subsequent chapter will provide a comprehensive analysis of several budgeting tools that will prove beneficial.

Make Luck Your Destiny:
Develop your character in such a manner that the role of chance transforms into a predictable outcome.
It is quite intriguing that the initial three forms of luck that I elucidated beforehand constitute widely recognized and familiar cliches. Furthermore, with regards to the fortuitous circumstances arising from one's distinct actions, there exists no conventional adage to encapsulate this exceptional phenomenon.
Therefore, the initial three categories encompass fortuitous circumstances referred to as "dumb luck" or "blind luck," signifying the first type of luck. The second type of luck pertains to the well-known adage of "fortune favors the bold." This refers to individuals who achieve luck by actively stirring the pot and demonstrating proactive behavior.

The third form of luck, as individuals express it, is the belief that "opportunity smiles upon those who are well-prepared."

However, regarding the fourth type of fortune, there lacks a prevailing aphorism that adequately captures the distinct nature of your conduct. I find this intriguing and potentially consequential. Moreover, it highlights the fact that individuals are not fully capitalizing on this particular stroke of luck, thus failing to leverage its potential to the extent they ought to.

In my opinion, beyond that juncture, the situation progressively assumes such a deterministic nature that fortuitous occurrences cease to play a significant role. Hence, the conceptualization gradually shifts from luck to a more prominent notion of destiny. Therefore, I would describe the fourth element as one's deliberate cultivation of character, wherein the individual's character ultimately shapes their future.

Cultivate your character in a manner that allows opportunities to gravitate towards you.

One aspect that I deem crucial in achieving financial success is cultivating a reputable image that entices individuals to engage in transactions with you. I exemplify the scenario where proficient divers are sought after by treasure seekers who reward them with a portion of the treasure in recognition of their diving prowess.

If you possess a reputation of being trustworthy, dependable, principled, and possessing a long-term vision as a negotiator, it is likely that individuals seeking to engage in deals but lacking the ability to establish trust with unknown parties will turn to you. In recognition of the credibility and standing you have diligently cultivated, they may offer you a share of the deal or propose an exclusive arrangement.

Warren Buffett, is approached with business opportunities, enabling him to acquire companies and warrants, and extend assistance to banks, leveraging his esteemed reputation to undertake actions beyond the reach of ordinary individuals.

Indeed, that is exceedingly delicate. It bears a sense of responsibility, it possesses a robust reputation, and as we will delve into further, it is accompanied by inherent responsibility.

However, it is my assertion that cultivating an esteemed character and preserving a reputable standing are endeavors enabling individuals to seize advantageous opportunities that others may perceive as fortuitous, despite recognizing them as products of deliberate actions rather than chance occurrences.

Yeah. Due to the heightened efficiency of the global landscape, individuals have extensively explored all obvious avenues. Therefore, in order to discover something truly innovative and uncharted, operating on the fringes becomes advantageous.

In such a location, it is necessary to possess a certain level of unconventional behavior in order to venture out onto the frontier unaccompanied. Furthermore, one must exhibit a propensity to delve into subjects more extensively than their counterparts, surpassing what may be considered rational, solely driven by a profound sense of curiosity.

Indeed, I have come across two quotes that effectively convey the concept of luck. One such quote, articulated by Sam Altman, states that "extreme individuals attain extraordinary outcomes." I find this notion to be quite profound and elegant. Furthermore, there is another perspective shared by Jeffrey Pfeffer, an esteemed professor at Stanford University, who asserts that one cannot attain extraordinary gains by adhering to conventional practices. I have consistently found this viewpoint to be enlightening as well.

One quote that I appreciate, which showcases an antithetical perspective, is as follows: "Engaging in foolish endeavors yields unsatisfactory outcomes." Numerous individuals invest ample time participating in social games, such as Twitter interactions, with the aim of augmenting their social status. However, these individuals merely obtain trivial social rewards that possess no real value.

The concept revolves around the notion that by actively pursuing various forms of luck, with the exception of merely coincidental luck, one inevitably depletes their reservoir of fortunate outcomes. So, if you just keep stirring the pot and stirring the pot, that alone you will run out of unluck.

It is possible that this is simply a return to the average. Therefore, one ensures that chance has no influence and that only one's abilities are significant.

2.2 Refrain from fixating on amassing monetary resources, but focus instead on acquiring wealth or assets.

One can possess significant wealth and still be indigent. This occurrence has been observed numerous times across various nations. It denotes a phenomenon known as hyperinflation. When Central Banks engage in large-scale monetary issuance, it can lead to a significant devaluation of the currency, rendering it virtually devoid of value.

Arguably the most notable instance occurred with the Hungarian Pengo, which was in circulation from 1927 to 1946. It experienced an exorbitantly high inflation rate of 41.9 quadrillion percent. There is no remainder of zero. There is a sequence of 14 consecutive zeros.

Upon initial observation, it appears evident that possessing a sum of 10 million units of any given currency (such as euro, dollar, pound, etc.) undoubtedly denotes wealth, and attaining a total of 1 billion is limited solely to a select few individuals, commonly referred to as billionaires. In Hungary during the year 1945, the price of one kilogram of bread amounted to a staggering six trillion pengos. Purchasing a single slice of bread would remain an unattainable feat even with the possession of 1 billion pengos.

Whomever possessed 6 trillion Hungarian pengos in the year 1927 would have been exceedingly affluent. Anyone who possessed 6 billion Hungarian pengos in 1946 was extremely impoverished. This is hyperinflation.

It is not an isolated incidence; Zimbabwe witnessed a scenario where individuals would have to carry a wheelbarrow filled with currency notes just to purchase a loaf of bread. Similarly, comparable circumstances were encountered in Germany during the 1920s, where approximately 4 trillion German marks were required to purchase 1 US dollar. Similar situations have also been observed in Poland, as well as several countries across South America and Asia.

Currency (banknotes, coins, checking accounts, etc.) represents merely one form of wealth and does not necessarily guarantee optimal or enduring security in the long term.

Excluding the aforementioned extreme scenarios, it is advisable to avoid relying on banknotes, coins, current accounts, and similar financial instruments as long-term investments. Neither in terms of financial gain nor in regards to safeguarding.

Financial resources are undeniably crucial and highly advantageous. However, I implore you to shift your focus towards accumulating assets, as it is the possession of assets that has the potential to truly transform your life, rather than the mere accumulation of money.

2.3 Primary manifestations or conditions of affluence

2.3.1 Banknotes and coins

Banknotes and coins are not a favorable method for wealth accumulation due to their inherent tendency to consistently depreciate in value.

They possess no inherent worth, serving merely as physical entities composed of paper and metal. They possess monetary status due to their agreed-upon acceptance, rather than inherent intrinsic worth. Paper and nickel, along with other contemporary materials used in coin production, are highly abundant in nature and possess negligible intrinsic worth.

It is intriguing that, for a considerable number of individuals, banknotes and coins hold the designation of "THE MONEY" in capitalized form, serving as the most secure method to safeguard their financial assets (disregarding any redundant aspect).

The long-term security provided by banknotes and coins is essentially synonymous with the risk of financial ruin. This decimation can manifest through a variety of mechanisms: Alternatively, the destruction can occur through multiple means:

Promptly, as a result of incidents such as theft, fire, loss, etc.

Gradually, due to the impact of inflation.

It is indisputable that impending destruction is approaching. In due course, yet it arrives.

However, it is commonly held that in the case of a significant economic catastrophe, only those individuals who possess physical currency will be "rescued." Nonetheless, historical evidence fails to support this notion as well. In the midst of significant economic crises, the individuals most adversely impacted typically encompass those in possession of physical currency, such as banknotes and coins. (Please take note: if a country were to be subjected to the establishment of a dictatorship, the circumstances would be distinct.) Under such circumstances, any valuable asset can be subject to expropriation or pilferage by those entrusted with enforcing the dictatorial regime. However, under those circumstances, it is apparent that we have shifted our focus away from economic risks and onto a different category altogether.

In numerous armed conflicts and comparable instances of grave circumstances, currency notes have been rendered invalid with immediate effect. To put it differently, the aforementioned objects have transformed from being considered as "currency" to mere physical elements of paper and metal that lack acceptance in exchange for goods or services. Individuals who possessed tangible assets such as real estate, shares, companies, jewellery, and other forms of wealth, retained possession of said assets on the subsequent day. Conversely, those individuals who solely possessed banknotes and coins were rendered destitute. In times of conflict, the physical structures on a property may incur destruction; however, the ownership of the land and the entitlement to reconstruct upon it remains vested in its proprietor.

Another scenario in which banknotes and coins are greatly affected is the hyperinflation that has been previously discussed. When the price of a loaf of bread undergoes a rapid increase from 1 unit to 1 billion units within a short span of time, the resulting consequence is the significant devaluation of banknotes, rendering their value nearly negligible. From a logical standpoint, this scenario proves detrimental to any asset; however, upon the restoration of normalcy, real estate, stocks, and similar assets persist as property of their rightful owners and retain (to a certain extent) their value. In contrast, obsolete banknotes and coins undergo a cessation of circulation, resulting in a complete loss of their value as they are supplanted by new currency.

In the event of a total collapse of a financial system, banknotes and coins would most likely lose all their value. This could occur due to either their removal from the circulation or the potential generation of hyperinflation. In the event of the funds in accounts and deposits being depleted, the tangible manifestations of currency, namely banknotes and coins, would likewise cease to exist. In light of current circumstances, it can be observed that these items primarily consist of economically viable materials such as inexpensive paper and metals, whose valuation is predominantly derived from the prevailing financial structures. Devoid of the support provided by these fiscal structures, those entities would possess minimal worth, akin to mere paper or inexpensive metals of little intrinsic value.

A developed nation is reliant upon a financial system for its sustenance. It is an exceedingly grave situation, making it uncertain as to what course of action would be pursued in the event of such circumstances. Firstly, this implies that the unlikelihood of such a scenario renders it economically disadvantageous to make provisions for it. In contrast, considering the inability to anticipate the strategies that would be implemented, it becomes arduous to ascertain beforehand whether the decision we are making is judicious or not. In any event, it is decidedly more effortless to nullify the worth of banknotes and coins, as opposed to altering the ownership of tangible properties and corporate entities.

Banknotes and coins serve as valuable means for covering modest day-to-day expenditures. They ought to persist in existence, and it is prudent to retain a sum in your possession for minor day-to-day expenditures. However, when considering them as a financial venture, it is advisable to abstain from engaging with them.

What Is Your Approach To Creating A Budget And Adhering To It?

If you are seeking to establish a personal budget, commence by undertaking these six sequential procedures

The majority of individuals necessitate a means by which they can monitor and record their financial activities on a monthly basis. A budget can provide you with a heightened perception of financial dominion and facilitate the accumulation of funds towards your objectives. Discovering a financial monitoring system that suits your needs is the key. With assistance from the following steps, it is possible to create a budget.

The initial step involves ascertaining your net income.

Your net income acts as the foundation for an effective budgeting strategy. Your net earnings encompass the total amount of compensation you receive after subtracting taxes and employer-provided benefits such as retirement plans and healthcare coverage. Directing your attention towards your gross pay as opposed to your net pay has the potential to lead to imprudent spending habits, as it may create a false perception of greater financial resources available to you. It is advised for individuals engaged in freelance work, gig economy, contracting, or self-employment to maintain comprehensive documentation of their contracts and compensation in order to effectively deal with fluctuating income.

Secondly, monitor your expenditures.

After calculating your income, it is essential to ascertain the destinations of your financial resources. By diligently monitoring and categorizing your expenses, you can ascertain your major expenditure sources and identify the areas where reductions in costs can be most conveniently implemented.

Begin by enumerating your non-variable expenditures. These comprise conventional monthly expenses such as payments for utilities and automobiles, as well as rent or mortgage payments, and so on. Subsequently, compile an inventory of your fluctuating expenditures, encompassing items such as groceries, fuel, and leisure activities that may vary on a monthly basis. There may be potential fiscal benefits to be found in this particular area. As credit card and bank statements often provide a detailed breakdown or categorization of your monthly expenditures, they serve as an advantageous starting point.

It is advisable to utilize any feasible means, such as writing instruments and paper, smartphone applications, or online budgeting spreadsheets or templates, in order to diligently monitor your day-to-day expenditures. Utilize any resources at hand, be it traditional tools like pen and paper, technological aids like smartphone applications, or digital budgeting spreadsheets and templates, to diligently monitor your expenditures on a daily basis.

Step 3: Formulate objectives that are strategic and achievable.

Prior to commencing the analysis of the compiled data, it is advisable to create a comprehensive catalogue of both immediate and enduring financial objectives. Short-term goals, achievable within a span of one to three years, may encompass endeavors such as establishing a contingency fund or diminishing outstanding credit card liabilities. Strategic goals such as devising a retirement plan or securing funds for your child's education often entail a time horizon spanning several decades. While it is not necessary for your goals to be immovable, having a clear understanding of them can serve as a motivating factor in adhering to your financial plan. For example, if you have the intention of saving for a vacation, it may be more convenient to decrease expenditures.

4. Create a plan

The convergence of factors lies in the distinction between actual expenditure and desired expenditure. To ascertain your anticipated expenditures for the forthcoming months, make use of the compiled catalog enumerating your fluctuating and constant financial obligations. Subsequently, compare this with your own set of priorities and overall income. Please give careful consideration to the implementation of clearly defined and achievable spending limits for each designated category of expenditure.

You may opt to further categorize your expenditures by delineating them into discretionary and essential expenses. If one commutes to work on a daily basis, for example, gasoline would be classified as a necessity. Nevertheless, a monthly music subscription could be regarded as a discretionary expense. This differentiation is of utmost importance when attempting to determine the reallocation of funds towards your financial objectives.

Step 5: Adjust your expenditure to align with your budget.

After properly documenting your income and expenditures, you can proceed to implement any necessary adjustments in order to avoid exceeding your budgetary limits and allocate funds towards your intended objectives. It would be advisable to prioritize reductions in discretionary expenses as the initial course of action. For instance, one might consider opting for in-home movie viewing instead of attending cinematic screenings. If you have already implemented modifications to your discretionary spending, it is advisable to scrutinize your monthly expenditures on payments. Upon further scrutiny, it is possible that a "need" could simply be categorized as something that is challenging to let go of.

If your calculations continue to lack coherence, it would be advisable to contemplate adjusting your fixed expenses. For instance, could you potentially achieve greater savings by conducting a thorough search for more favorable options in terms of homeowners' or auto insurance? Consider your options meticulously as significant concessions are associated with such decisions.

It is important to note that even small savings can accumulate to a significant amount. Gradually making minor modifications can result in a substantial accumulation of additional funds.

Step 6: Regularly evaluate your budget

After establishing your budget, it is of utmost importance to consistently monitor both your budget and expenditures to ensure you are maintaining adherence to your financial plan. There are few items within your budget that can be regarded as definite.

As an illustration, the expenses could potentially fluctuate, an increase in salary may arise, or the achievement of an objective might prompt the establishment of fresh targets. Regardless of the underlying cause, it is imperative to establish a consistent habit of engaging in regular budget reviews through the utilization of the aforementioned protocols.

3. Develop and adhere to a financial plan or budget.

Therefore, you may wish to commence strategizing, lest you are required to exercise more efficient financial management strategies than ever before. You do not require subjective figures on a financial record; instead, you necessitate a devised scheme for your expenditures that you can steadfastly adhere to, thus enabling you to effectively manage your finances with certainty.

First and foremost, allow me to express my admiration. Such a decision necessitates great courage. We are content with your performance. Furthermore, you will adhere to your financial plan—it merely necessitates effort to establish a rational and logical financial plan. We need to establish the method by which you will initiate that process.

What is the rationale behind adhering to your financial plan?

Tune in. You possess lofty aspirations and ambitions—destinations to journey to and goals to achieve. Furthermore, you will be immersed in the nourishment as well. . . Nevertheless, it is essential to initiate the process with a carefully crafted financial plan. What kind of expenditure can have detrimental consequences if it is set and forgotten? Your objectives are certainly not akin to a slow cooker, and your budget does not align with it either. You cannot simply input numbers, press a button, and walk away. You must persist and remain persevering.

Developing a financial strategy involves taking responsibility for managing your funds. Demonstrating adherence to the financial plan indicates your accountability towards your funds. The most optimal approach to adhere to your financial plan is through the practice of budgeting.

There exist numerous strategies and tactics to effectively adhering to your monthly budget. However, using the term "tons" beyond a certain limit can be deemed excessive. We have selectively narrowed it down to a final selection of the top eight options:

1. Keep it genuine.

Have you ever pursued a goal or objective that ultimately led to disappointment? Similar to stating that, you will diligently consume ten books per month despite having minimal remaining energy. Alternatively, making a commitment to consistently complete a ten-mile run every day throughout the entirety of the year without any prior experience in running even a single meter. If you aspire to achieve success, it is imperative to push yourself, while also maintaining a pragmatic approach.

The equivalence holds true in accordance with your budgetary constraints. Take initiative to enhance your expenditure habits and increase your savings. However, it is essential to exercise prudence once you have evaluated every expense category. Declaring that you will decline any new garments throughout the entire year would not be prudent, especially considering that your winter coat is deteriorating. Nevertheless, you will have the opportunity to refrain from frequenting cafes for a duration of one month and allocate the funds you would have spent towards your immediate financial goal instead.

When you maintain authenticity, you will truly achieve success.

2. Discovered Auto Draft.

Erect automated bank drafts to facilitate the direct payment of certain bills and investment funds from your paycheck. Therefore, at that juncture, you refrain from contacting the funds for a sufficient duration so as to avoid the temptation of allocating that $200 to purchasing a new pair of shoes that you desire, but do not necessarily require.

3. Plan your dinners.

Outperform tempting drive-through offers that exceed your restaurant budget, and retain financial control over indulgent expenditures. Accomplish this by meticulously organizing your meals, encompassing breakfast, lunch, dinner, and snacks. Subsequently, compile a comprehensive grocery list and adhere strictly to it. By engaging in meal planning, you safeguard against excessive expenditures in both grocery shopping and dining out.

4. Think week after week.

You may find it necessary to reallocate some of your expenditure categories into weekly segments in order to create more financial flexibility. For instance, if an allocation of $200 is made for personal expenses, it would be prudent to regard this as $50 per week. If you allocate $894 in your average monthly budget for essential groceries (which is the standard expenditure for a household of four), it would equate to an expenditure of approximately $223 per week. From time to time, contemplating these condensed amounts facilitates adherence to your monetary plan.

5. Deliberately examine your social agenda.

Your best friend's birthday occurs on the same day every year. Permit it. You will be overseeing the book club event in a month's time and would like to arrange a curated selection of cured meats and cheeses on a wooden serving platter. Permit it. Relatives are arriving from out of town. You get the idea.

Certainly, unforeseen circumstances and remarkable events may arise that will significantly impact your financial resources. However, the occurrence of what we commonly refer to as "shocks" can often be attributed to a significant lack of anticipation and foresight. In a similar vein, it is advisable to examine your social commitments while formulating your monthly financial plan, ensuring that you allocate funds prudently to meet all your ongoing needs.

Moreover, please be at ease. There is no need for you to construct each budget entirely from scratch. Review the content previously covered, and subsequently modify only the budget categories that will undergo any forthcoming changes.

6. Determine the Appropriate Terminology for Absence or Non-Existence.

If you happen to have an inclination to pursue a certain objective, a limited financial capacity does not necessarily imply a complete negation. However, it often suggests a postponement, with the intention to allocate resources towards larger expenditures and financial obligations. In addition, truthfully, on certain occasions, one must indeed express a negative response. That exemplifies the responsibilities associated with adulthood. You cannot recklessly progress and obtain everything you desire. Similar to forgoing social gatherings, thus conserving both your energy and time. The same principle applies to abstaining from occasional expenditures; refraining from spending ensures the preservation of your financial resources and secures your future financial stability.

Do not excessively concern yourself with what individuals across various social media platforms appear to possess. A number of individuals are not being truthful. Certain individuals are diligently reimbursing their creditors to the extent of their architectural obligations. Additionally, it is worth noting that many individuals indeed foster harmonious coexistence. Regardless, those individuals diligently persevered through it—and that is precisely what you are being afforded the opportunity to do as well.

Take a resolute stance in overseeing your budget—exercising restraint by declining or deferring purchases—since prioritizing your self-discipline, financial plan, and monetary aspirations supersedes any potential acquisition.

7. Trench The MasterCard.

Exercise prudence and be mindful that possessing a Master Card does not facilitate adherence to your financial plan. To be frank, it is commonplace for individuals to endure immense difficulties while holding the belief that such trials foreshadow future challenges.

Hello. Think about what. The forthcoming matter may serve as an inadequate excuse, and you are of higher stature than that!

In the eventuality of your preference to adhere to your budgetary limitations, it is advisable to refrain from utilizing borrowed funds that may be burdened with interest charges. Employ your legitimate funds—your cash or credit card. This is the approach to avoid being left behind by the implications of "the forthcoming matters" and begin pursuing the forthcoming goals.

8. Discover A Spending Mate.

Ensure that you receive exceptional planning assistance by acquiring a financial partner, referred to as a responsibility accomplice. That individual is deeply comforting and abundantly spirited, capable of providing support and offering constructive criticism. Got a companion? Blast. You possess an innate inclination to spend.

Engage in regular communication with your financial partner on a monthly basis in order to assess and ascertain the ensuing budget. If you are married, it is advisable to conduct a monthly financial meeting together, ensuring mutual participation and collaboration. If you are collaborating with a significant or beloved individual, you have the autonomy to establish your budget independently; however, do not neglect the process of consultation. Your companion cannot hold you accountable if they are unaware of the circumstances.

Should you find yourself unsure of how to effectively manage expenses together with your financial partner on a monthly basis, we recommend acquiring a copy of our comprehensive one-page budgeting meeting guide (available in both the classic and couple's editions).

Please be aware that there is no shame in seeking assistance to maintain focus on the objective. Simply the other. The pursuit of accountability harbors boundless fortitude. Therefore, I suggest acquiring a financial companion for managing your expenditures. Today!

Strategizing Allocations For Expenditure On Mental Health

In terms of expenditure on mental health, I propose implementing an A/B budget arrangement. The A budget is applicable in scenarios wherein one's mental well-being is enhanced, and there is no necessity to depend on supplementary expenditures for support.

The B budget would encompass the incorporation of supplementary measures and slightly curtail expenditure in order to bolster savings.

Allocate a portion of your monthly funds exclusively to cover mental health expenses, ensuring their availability when required.

Please ensure that you continue to differentiate between impulsive spending driven by emotions and the importance of maintaining good mental well-being. Emotional expenditure can be likened to a mere attempt at superficially addressing underlying issues, whereas allocation of funds towards mental health endeavors serves as a strategic investment in effectively navigating feelings of being overwhelmed.

2) Determine the Factors that Prompt Your Expenditures

There exist numerous factors that lead to our expenditures and an array of stimuli that prompt us to engage in spending behavior.

We are experiencing joy, and therefore we desire to commemorate this occasion.

We are burdened by a sense of guilt, thus it is our intention to compensate our friend who graciously settled our expenses on the previous occasion.

We are experiencing a state of ennui and are seeking immediate engagement.

Many of these triggers are ultimately attributed to fatigue and the pressures of daily life. In periods characterized by fatigue and high levels of stress, these expenditure patterns become ingrained routines. Our propensity for fiscal excess begins to adopt a habitual nature.

How can one undertake the task of identifying these triggers?

Allocate a few weeks to engage in reflective writing, documenting both your expenditures and the corresponding emotional impact they have on you. Please allocate a few moments of your day to respond to three inquiries pertaining to your expenditures: what were the emotions experienced at the instance of each transaction? And what is your current emotional state in regards to your purchase?

Make an effort to discern recurring patterns in your conduct and identify areas where you tend to overspend.

Do you allocate a greater amount of funds on specific days of the week?

When one is in the company of a specific assemblage of individuals

Enhance your clarity and precision regarding your triggers.

This constitutes the initial phase. If one lacks awareness regarding the reasons and timing behind their expenditures, they will find themselves grappling with an imperceptible influence.

3) Redirect Your Emotional Catalysts

Now that you are cognizant of the underlying causes for your emotional spending, or at the very least have compiled a comprehensive list of such reasons, it becomes imperative to identify alternative channels through which such patterns can be redirected.

Upon careful reflection, it has come to my attention that redirecting financial resources towards emotional well-being predominantly hinges upon comprehending the significance and worth of engaging in self-care practices.

Given the intricacy of our emotions, our behavior tends to deteriorate when we are fatigued and depleted.

Initially, it is imperative to establish a foundation of consistent self-care.

How do you ensure adequate rest, maintain a nutritious diet, and allocate sufficient time for indulging in activities you are passionate about? Devise a strategy to allocate additional time for personal pursuits within your daily agenda.

Commence with modest steps; establishing novel habits can prove challenging, yet the resultant transformation undoubtedly yields immense value.

In addition, compile a roster of activities that you can engage in during moments of emotional distress, when the inclination to indulge in excessive expenditure arises.

Journal. Please venture outdoors and engage in a leisurely stroll. Initiate contact with a friend. Engage in a brief, five-minute celebratory dance session accompanied by a song of your choice. Ensure that you maintain a regularly visible record of your grounding exercises, allowing for prompt engagement with these activities before resorting to online shopping platforms such as Amazon or Etsy.

In the final analysis, material possessions are unlikely to alleviate one's stress or enhance one's sense of worth.

5. Embrace Change - Provide your child with a financial advantage

Numerous caretakers contend that engaging in discussions with their offspring regarding financial matters presents an undeniable challenge. The theme is perceived as unduly fragile or they simply lack the confidence to provide valuable insights. In any event, the most unfavorable example that any parent could ever provide a child concerning money is refraining from discussing it.

Children benefit greatly from the example they are provided, making it crucial to demonstrate that money should not evoke fear or anxiety in them. Cash should be utilized to generate benefits.

Engage them in the management of their savings

Are they cognizant of the fact that you are setting aside funds for their education? Are they fully aware of your regular financial management, including the allocation and purpose of the funds? Revealing to your children that you are setting aside funds for their future permits you to engage in a dialogue regarding the significance of this action and its mechanics.

This will not only engender a sense that they cannot simply appropriate things without consequence.

Permitted, nevertheless it also prompts them to contemplate the importance of financial planning.

Consider their future prior to them doing so.

The earlier individuals commence safeguarding funds for their retirement, the lesser the required amount of their savings will be. Arguably, the most significant impact you can have on their future financial well-being is, therefore, to initiate on their behalf. Consider allocating a lump sum to your adolescent upon reaching the age of either eighteen or twenty-one, to be deposited into their tax-exempt account or invested in a retirement fund.

Despite not perceiving your contribution as significant, an initial sum of R10 000 will grow to nearly R1 million over a span of 45 years, given an annual growth rate of 10%.

This will provide a valuable boost to their future retirement prospects and also prompt them to contemplate their financial future as they embark on their professional journey. Presuming this is done within a retirement annuity (RA) structure, access to the funds can only be granted once the individual reaches a minimum age of 55. This ensures that the funds are appropriately reserved for their intended purpose.

Nevertheless, if you are willing to agree that they will be dedicated, it is justified to utilize a tax-exempt banking account. This is due to the fact that over an extended period of time, the advantages of a tax-exempt bank account are likely to be greater, and you can also invest fully in growth assets such as equities, whereas a retirement annuity must adhere to the restrictions imposed by Regulation 28 (The legislation ensuring that South African retirement savings are managed prudently and with diversification)."

Africans make careful and strategic contributions to their retirement, ensuring the growth and preservation of their retirement funds, while also directing their investments towards achieving financial development and prosperity.

Similar to all investment funds, the earlier you commence making preparations for this, the more advantageous it will be. If you consistently allocate R100 from the moment your child is born, you will have accumulated savings amounting to R21,600 by the time they reach the age of 18. If we presume a 10% annual growth rate for this portfolio, the approximate amount that could be bestowed upon them would exceed R60,000.

It is possible to accomplish this by establishing a tax-exempt bank account from the onset, whereby you can initiate an account in the name of your child. You also have the option to initiate the opening of a Registered Account (RA).

Engage with them during their early years (yet they will not gain any benefit from the tax-deductible contributions).

Alternatively, to provide them with monetary funds in a Registered Account (RA), invest resources in a unit trust until the point at which you wish to provide them with the lump sum, and subsequently transfer it into a RA at the time when they become financially independent adults and can benefit from the tax deduction.

Fostering a culture of savings among our children is a strategy aimed at ensuring their financial security during retirement. To ensure the development of sound savings habits in a young individual, it is incumbent upon us as parents to provide guidance in imparting fundamental investment principles and fostering an understanding of the underlying rationale for saving.

Engaging our children in relevant discussions with financial planners and involving them in financial deliberations - as deemed appropriate for their age - will facilitate their comprehension of the overarching perspective as they witness the growth of their funds.

The majority of individuals will agree that the earlier we commence saving for retirement, the easier it is to achieve our financial objectives, and the more uncomplicated it becomes to accumulate the required amount on a regular basis. It would be accurate to infer that commencing saving during the early stages of one's life would facilitate a smoother financial journey.

Additionally, an individual who initiates the practice of saving from an early age is likely to cultivate favorable savings habits and exhibit consistent savings behavior throughout their adult life.

Instilling in children the understanding that they also have the potential to amass wealth through adopting a judicious investment strategy can serve as a compelling source of motivation.

Children greatly benefit from a consistent schedule: even small regular activities can have a substantial cumulative effect over time due to the power of compounding. Despite the tangible financial value held in a RA account, our children will benefit additionally from cultivating prudent financial habits. Many financial experts and educators posit that an early initiation into financial literacy increases the likelihood of future financial stability.

Registered Accounts (RA's) are highly recognized within the adult investor community, but they also serve as exceptional means of savings for children who, due to their young age, are in an advantageous position to leverage time and the compounding effect. Providing our children with Registered Accounts (RA) not only grants them a significant head start in saving for retirement, but also imparts invaluable financial knowledge.

With even the slightest commitment, a conservative registered advisor (RA) is able to provide a platform for our children to learn about charges, retirement planning, compounding, and the interplay between earning, saving, and expenditure. While concerns about retirement benefits may likely be the final thought in their youthful minds, many children are captivated by the notion that a modest investment in the present can yield substantial financial gains in the future.

Although young children may not fully grasp the concepts of revenue, income, and building, their level of maturity enables them to appreciate the potential for their money to grow. As children progress towards adulthood and eventually enter the workforce, their annual contributions are likely to increase, consequently resulting in the potential growth of the RA. By consistently setting aside funds on a monthly or annual basis for a RA, even if the contributions are modest, we can instill in our children a sense of financial responsibility and nurture a prudent approach towards money management.

If your child is a legal minor, specifically under 18 years of age, it is advisable to establish a custodial or guardian-based Registered Account (RA). In your capacity as the custodian, you (as the responsible party) maintain control over the assets held in the custodial RA until your child attains the age of 18, at which juncture the assets shall be transferred to him or her. The Registered Account (RA) is established under the name of your minor, requiring you to provide their identification number upon initiating the account.

Provide gifts that hold significance.

Evidently, children possess an inherent fondness for toys, relishing the joy that arises from engaging with playthings. Nevertheless, it is not imperative for every gift they receive to instill instantaneous gratification. Investing money in a unit trust or opening a stockbroking account may not be perceived as the most remarkable present in the world, but it can yield considerable benefits.

Firstly, it imparts to individuals a sense of possessing their own financial resources and having some funds at their disposal. Over time, it is also the most optimal approach to familiarize them with various savings products, asset categories, as well as concepts such as revenue and profits, as they can witness firsthand their functionalities.

An affordable online brokerage account would also empower them to exercise autonomy in making investment decisions regarding the stocks they wish to invest in. In their early years, their choices may not be guided by comprehensive scrutiny, Nonetheless, they can still invest in companies that they possess some knowledge about.

As an illustration, if they happen to have a preference for Spur, Nandos, or McDonalds as dining options, why not showcase to them the opportunity of acquiring a stake in those establishments? Alternatively, if you typically conduct your shopping at Pick n Pay, Shoprite, or Woolworths, let them be responsible for acquiring the shares.

As time progresses, it is highly likely that individuals will gain a comprehensive understanding of how these organizations function, their revenue generation processes, and the implications involved in being an investor. This will ultimately result in them making more informed decisions regarding their investment choices.

Maintaining A Fiscal Balance By Expending Below One's Income.

The distinction between the affluent and the less privileged is as follows: the wealthy allocate their funds towards investments and utilize the remainder for expenditure. Those with a lower socioeconomic status allocate their funds toward immediate expenses and commit the remaining amount to financial investments - Robert Kiyosaki
The amount you can save is contingent upon multiple factors and will fluctuate on a monthly basis. However, there exists a fundamental principle that must not be neglected if attaining financial independence is your desired goal.
It is imperative to ensure that your expenditure remains within the limits of your income.
Individuals who consistently surpass their income through excessive spending find themselves fully immersed in the

relentless pursuit of material success and often resort to seeking loans in order to afford desired expenditures. Automotive financing, vacation financing, and even television financing have become prevalent across various sectors, with the root cause being insufficient savings resulting from excessive expenditure surpassing one's income.

My personal objective is to optimize monthly savings. The fixed amount is not predetermined due to occasional unexpected expenses that may lead to increased spending, while some months are uneventful resulting in reduced expenditures. Nevertheless, I consistently allocate a portion of my income towards savings. There are certain months during which I manage to allocate half of my salary towards savings, while in other months, my savings are limited to merely 10%. However, it is worth emphasizing that I maintain a consistent habit of saving.

Nevertheless, there are individuals who employ a highly advocated strategy in which they prioritize savings before indulging in expenditures. The key is to decide how much you want to save, for example 20% of the salary and transfer it directly to the savings account just when it's cashed, forcing you to pass the month with the remaining amount and forcing you to save money. The magnitude of your withdrawal may appear challenging to attain, as commencing with a low amount would result in foregoing potential savings. Commence from a superior level and decrease if obtaining it proves unattainable, rather than the reverse.

If you happen to be an individual prone to unrestrained spending habits and a lack of consistent saving, I strongly advise employing this strategic approach to witness the advantageous outcomes it yields.

Due to the consistent accumulation of funds on a monthly basis, pertaining to the purchases of vehicles, televisions, or vacations, there will be no requirement to seek financial assistance as the necessary funds will already be readily available.

Credits and loans

The encumbrance of obligations can be likened to a form of servitude experienced by those who are otherwise at liberty - Publius Syrus

Utilizing credit to sustain an extravagant lifestyle has become a prevalent trend among individuals entrenched in the pursuit of success, yet it is imperative to eschew such practices as they invariably yield inflated costs for every purchase made on borrowed funds.

Two decades ago, individuals sought financial assistance in the form of a loan to acquire residential properties, commonly with a repayment term of ten years, which was considered a reasonable length of time. In the past, individuals would cultivate their savings to acquire televisions, computers, or indulge in vacations, a practice that is increasingly becoming obsolete in contemporary times.

In earlier times, individuals who lacked financial means to embark on vacations simply refrained from doing so, thereby conserving expenses and, potentially, enabling future travel in the subsequent year. In contemporary times, individuals who are unable to embark on a vacation face no difficulty in obtaining loans for this purpose, thereby not only expending funds they lack, but also incurring substantial interest fees.

Purchases made on credit incur a significantly higher monetary expense. Real examples.

Upon careful examination of the prevailing loan terms in the market, it becomes apparent that purchasing on credit incurs significant additional expenses. Here are two examples.

Example 1. Automobile financing extended by a financial institution.

An individual desiring to purchase a car may consider obtaining a loan from a bank, as financial institutions often provide more favorable terms compared to numerous online platforms that extend loans devoid of conditions or inquiries. In the given scenario, where your intention is to procure $10,000 for the purpose of purchasing a vehicle, you approach a financial institution in order to obtain a loan, subject to the subsequent terms and conditions identified as the prevailing market average.

A sum of ten thousand dollars.

The duration of repayment spans 60 months.

The monthly installment amounts to $200.

Compulsory premium payments

The annual percentage rate is 10.45%.

The total sum to be reimbursed is $12,580.

Consequently, the purchase of a $10,000 automobile through a loan featuring conditions that are relatively favorable in comparison to prevailing market rates, amounts to a total of $12,580, representing a 25.8% increase.

How can an individual who lacks the means to accumulate $10,000 for the purchase of a vehicle subsequently manage to afford a payment of $12,580?

Under these circumstances, in a sound and judicious manner, it would be advisable, in my personal view, to allocate 50 months towards the accumulation of $200, rather than directing the same time frame towards repayment over 60 months, due to the substantial interest disparity. Concurrently, one could consider acquiring a pre-owned vehicle or retaining their current one. As an illustration, my automobile, which has surpassed 15 years in its existence, shall remain in my possession until its functionality ceases, despite my capacity to acquire a new one without reliance on any form of financial assistance.

Example 2. A personal loan devoid of inquiries or requisites typically found on conventional online platforms.
Financial institutions typically extend loans based on specific criteria, such as stable employment, for instance, though alternative funding options are also available for consideration. Individuals who are not granted approval for a loan

by financial institutions may consider seeking assistance from online platforms that offer smaller loans, typically amounting to approximately $6,000, often without stringent requirements. However, it is important to note that such alternatives tend to incur significantly higher costs as they carry greater risks associated with loan defaults.

These loans are frequently utilized to cover minor expenses such as televisions, mobile phones, holidays, and even to meet basic needs.

Allow us to examine a scenario wherein an individual seeks a sum of $3,000 for any of the aforementioned circumstances.

The cost is three thousand dollars.

The duration for repayment spans a period of 41 months.

The monthly payment is set at $105.

The annual percentage rate is 24.5%.

The aggregate sum to be reimbursed is $4305.

In this particular scenario, the act of obtaining a loan of $3,000 entails the responsibility of repaying a sum of $4,305 over a period of 41 months, amounting to an alarming additional interest of 43.5%. An individual who is unable to amass $3,000 for discretionary purposes should refrain from borrowing in this manner, as it will ultimately require them to shoulder an additional 43.5% burden, a task that will prove exceedingly arduous.

Upon entering the realm of purchasing goods through credit, the pricing of commodities takes a steep incline, creating a multifaceted conundrum that is arduous to escape. Hence, the most prudent approach would be to strive to evade this circumstance entirely, as per Kiyosaki, who refers to this perpetual cycle as the rat race. If an individual lacks the financial means to afford a $2,000 family vacation, it is indicative of their inability to accumulate savings. Hence, it would be unwise for them to procure a loan, subsequently incurring $3,000 in expenses for the very same holiday.

Once you have become entrenched within this cycle, it is imperative to exert a concerted endeavor in order to extricate oneself, as doing so will significantly ameliorate your financial situation. Despite the inherent sacrifice it entails, allocating time to postpone purchasing desired items or opting for more affordable alternatives can yield increased financial capacity for future acquisitions.

Living in a state of indebtedness can liken to servitude; thus, the foremost endeavor in attaining financial autonomy should entail the eradication of debts, particularly the conventional small loans characterized by exorbitant interest rates.

Instances of modest accumulations of savings.

It is most advantageous to commence by refraining from verbal communication and proceeding with action - Walt Disney.

It is essential to engage in savings, even through modest sums, in order to liberate oneself from financial dependence and attain a state of fiscal autonomy.

If excessive expenditures on unnecessary items are prevalent in your financial habits, initiating the practice of saving shall likely prove effortless. Conversely, for those already engaged in the virtuous act of saving, who perceive the task to be insurmountable, despondency is not warranted; I harbor confidence in your ability to conceive alternative methods to augment your savings. Consistently economizing on minor expenses, which may appear trivial, can accumulate significant savings over time, thereby emphasizing the importance of avoiding any notion that savings are inconsequential or unnecessary.

There exist numerous methodologies for budgeting and in this chapter, we will explore several illustrations. It may not be feasible to save in every instance we encounter, but it is crucial to endeavor and make an attempt to save in certain cases, an accomplishment that can be perfectly realized.

I wish to emphasize that I am a resident of Spain (specifically Mallorca), and as a result, the expenses I incur within this particular category will be influenced by this geographical context. In the event that certain items carry a higher price tag in your particular situation, this circumstance presents an advantageous opportunity to accumulate greater savings.

Saving in cars

Possessing a motor vehicle is frequently deemed a prerequisite and a possession that only a limited number of individuals are able or willing to relinquish. Regrettably, it stands as one of the most notable financial burdens within the realm of domestic economics.

The mean number of automobiles per household aligns more closely with 2 than with 1, resulting in significant inflation of household expenditures within this segment. Given the inherent challenges associated with not owning a car within a family unit, the prospect of minimizing the number of automobiles, particularly if multiple are currently possessed, represents a highly compelling and financially advantageous alternative.

Choosing a Broker

The majority of brokers provide different iterations of the aforementioned choices, namely mutual funds, stocks, bonds, options, and exchange-traded funds. Furthermore, certain establishments facilitate access to trading in currencies and futures.

The selection of a broker is contingent upon one's individual priorities. For instance, certain investors place cost as their utmost priority, while others are willing to incur high commissions due to their appreciation for the utilization of a contemporary platform. When selecting a brokerage, various factors necessitate thoughtful consideration and a modest amount of research. When you are prepared to assess brokers, it is important to consider five key factors: account fees, account minimums, trading

style and requirements, commissions, and promotions.
Account Fees

It is feasible to decrease account fees, and the potential benefits should not be overlooked. For instance, it is probable that Broker A will impose charges for actions such as the closure of your account and the transfer of funds to Broker B; however, Broker B may be open to providing compensation.

In the majority of instances, the most effective approach to circumvent broker fees is to opt for a broker that does not impose them. Several brokers incorporate service fees for items such as trading platform subscriptions, but if you do not intend to utilize them, you may have the option to opt out. Other fees
Such expenses can quickly accumulate, encompassing additional costs for research, fees related to inactivity, and annual charges. When contemplating a broker that entails additional charges, it

is essential to incorporate those sums into your assessments when evaluating alternatives.

If you have foreseen engaging in the trading of bonds, funds, or options, it is of utmost importance that you thoroughly assess the comprehensive price list of brokers. The inclusion of contract fees in addition to commission fees may indicate an excessive expenditure on your part.
Please ensure that you take into consideration the minimum account requirements.

Certain brokers and mutual funds mandate an initial investment that satisfies a minimum requirement. In the absence of effective strategies, it can pose potential challenges when commencing with limited financial resources, as the foremost objective becomes the successful allocation of said funds. Moreover, it is not arduous to locate trustworthy brokers that do not have any minimum account requirements. Several notable instances include Merrill Edge, Ally Invest, and TD Ameritrade.

Take into account your individual trading approach

One might perhaps not perceive an immediate necessity for an advanced trading platform; however, it is advisable to acquire knowledge in this domain. If you are perusing the websites of prospective brokers, search for any instructional materials or video presentations that they may offer. Brokerages frequently offer complimentary seminars to account-holders. Make use of these tools, even if you believe you do not require them. The majority of brokers provide their own ratings, while a subset offer the opportunity to access data from third-party sources such as Morningstar and Standard & Poor's.

A diligent trader should endeavor to find a broker that is in accordance with his or her intended level of activity. When conducting an analysis on various brokers, it is crucial to evaluate their provided analysis tools and trading platforms. There exists an ample selection of reliable brokers that permit complimentary access to research, tools, and trading platforms. Therefore, exercise caution when encountering a broker who levies additional fees for these services. These fees accumulate quickly.

If one is interested in engaging in trades on international exchanges, it will be necessary to undertake currency conversion. Certain brokers provide this as a potential choice; it is advisable to inquire about the prospect of converting your funds into international currencies.

Certain brokerages offer individuals the opportunity to evaluate the functionality of their software and applications prior to initiating account openings. In today's modern era, the paramount importance of accessibility has been acknowledged by brokerages, who are fully cognizant of the fact that customers are constantly in motion. It is advisable to peruse reviews of their mobile applications in order to determine if they align well with your personal preferences and lifestyle.

The appealing aspect of a mobile application lies in its convenience; nevertheless, it may be desirable to have the alternative of a physical branch establishment where personalized investment advice can be obtained. Many prominent brokerages typically maintain regional branches where clients can engage directly with financial advisors. In a broader sense, should your brokerage be institutionally affiliated with a bank, you will be afforded the opportunity to establish a link between your checking account and your brokerage account. This facilitates expedient and effortless monetary transactions. There may also be supplementary benefits to consider; it is prudent to investigate whether or not your existing bank has any affiliations with a brokerage firm.

ESSENTIAL ENTREPRENEURIAL SKILLS TO ACQUIRE

In addition to conducting thorough research and developing a comprehensive business plan, it is essential to consistently strive to acquire specific sets of skills that will contribute to the successful management of your business. If you do not possess a business degree, there is no need to be concerned. There exists a multitude of enterprising individuals who have effectively established prosperous enterprises without possessing a Master of Business Administration degree. However, they remained devoted to acquiring entrepreneurial expertise through alternative channels, such as perusing literature on business, participating in workshops, or enrolling in brief online educational programs.

In order to enhance the likelihood of achieving success, it is imperative to consistently enhance your repertoire of skills by acquiring a combination of technical proficiency and interpersonal abilities. Hard skills encompass the analytical and technical aptitudes that facilitate effective management of one's burgeoning enterprise, whereas soft skills pertain to the interpersonal competencies that foster the establishment of stronger business alliances. Herein lies a compilation of both tangible and intangible proficiencies that are imperative for you to consistently enhance as a leader:

1. Business Management

Acquiring and honing business management abilities is essential among the fundamental skills that must be acquired and cultivated. As a leader, it is incumbent upon you to oversee the daily operations of your enterprise and establish effective mechanisms that foster the expansion and development of your business. The acquisition of business management competencies equips individuals with the ability to formulate robust business strategies, identify avenues for enhancing profitability, and proficiently oversee the expansion of their workforce.

2. Leadership

The utilization of leadership skills enhances the efficacy of business management, as effective leadership encompasses more than mere affability. It is crucial to possess effective communication skills in order to effectively mentor your team and facilitate their growth within their designated positions. Leadership abilities are additionally advantageous in establishing a clear vision and fostering a conducive atmosphere within your organization, thereby ensuring the high levels of motivation necessary for your team to thrive.

3. Communication

You establish the precedent in terms of the degree of internal transparency and external openness that you attain, both within your organization and towards the customers you cater to. When possessing exceptional communication abilities, it ensures that all individuals within your organization, regardless of their hierarchical position, have a clear comprehension of their respective roles and responsibilities. Effective communication skills are also essential for effectively conveying your vision through branding and marketing materials, thereby enabling you to successfully engage with your desired target audience.

4. Customer Service

The clientele is vital to the sustenance of your enterprise. Your business's growth is contingent upon their presence. Every individual customer displays unique characteristics and expects to be treated with utmost attention and thoughtfulness during their interactions with your organization. Possessing adept customer service skills can facilitate the cultivation of a customer-centric enterprise, wherein every operational procedure or mechanism places paramount importance on catering to the customer's requirements. Additionally, you have the opportunity to refine your skills in the areas of cold calling, email marketing, and effectively managing dissatisfied customers through online platforms or telephone communication.

5. Finance

It is imperative for every entrepreneur to possess fundamental financial literacy in order to effectively manage their business finances, develop financial projections, generate invoices, and capitalize on opportunities to optimize their profits. Fortunately, start-up enterprises have the option to employ bookkeeping software for the purpose of efficiently managing their financial records. Nevertheless, it remains essential for entrepreneurs to possess the knowledge required to comprehend and evaluate financial statements, along with the necessary skills to properly file tax returns.

6. Critical Thinking

Critical thinking entails the capacity to employ reasoning and search for sound empirical support while formulating assertions or engaging in the process of navigating challenges. As an individual engaged in entrepreneurship, it is crucial to acquire the skill of evaluating information from diverse angles in order to devise comprehensive business strategies that encompass numerous variables and generate optimal resolutions.

7. Time Management

Every plan or strategy that is put into operation must adhere to a predetermined timeline. This timeline ensures that tasks are completed with a suitable tempo to attain your organizational goals. Lack of deadlines precludes the ability to formulate key projections and advance business growth. Effective time management skills facilitate the organization of one's time, enabling the timely completion of tasks within the predetermined timeframe. Additionally, they have the capacity to enhance business efficiency and facilitate the adaptability to market demands.

The Favorable Impacts Of Possessing A Credit Card

Upon establishing a positive payment history with the bank, your account will be automatically considered for renewal and potentially an increase in your current limit following an evaluation process. The sole method to ensure this outcome is by consistently making payments and occasionally settling the complete balance on the credit card.

Practicing effective credit card management contributes to the enhancement of your Credit Score.

It constitutes a prolonged line of credit that typically has a duration ranging from one (1) to four (4) years, after which it typically becomes invalid. In essence, this implies that you have access to a loan with a duration ranging from one to four years.

It serves as a contingency for lacking liquid funds, or it functions as a cushion during a phase of financial hardship.

Utilizing a credit card enables you to engage in online overseas transactions that may not be feasible or accessible through a debit card.

It serves as a viable contingency plan for travel purposes.

Instructions for Credit Card Activation

Upon receipt of your credit card by mail, you proceed to open the corresponding letter and proceed to activate the card as per the instructions provided therein. This correspondence typically indicates your assigned credit limit, and it is customary for your card to be enclosed within. PS. Your card is non-operational until it has been properly activated.

The obligatory fees linked to a credit card following its activation and initial usage.

Charge applied by the MSDE (expressed as a percentage) to the remaining balance

Late Payment Penalty - A predetermined sum levied upon failure to meet the designated payment deadline or remit an amount below the stipulated minimum.

Example:

If the prescribed sum amounts to $5530, the stipulated due date for payment is May 30th, 20xx.

If you fail to remit the payment of $5500 by May 30th, 20xx, you will incur a late payment fee of $30 for the aforementioned amount overlooked. Please be sure to remit the total amount indicated on your invoice.

Yearly Membership Fee - A predetermined sum imposed upon you for the advantage of possessing the card. You are required to remit this sum.

The "Over-the-Limit Fee" is a fixed sum of money that you will incur once you surpass the pre-approved credit limit assigned to your credit card.

Strategies for surpassing your Credit Card Limit;

You reach the credit limit on your card and then the (MSDE) interest is computed and subsequently applied to the balance.

You failed to make the payment for your credit card when the card was already nearing its maximum credit utilization.

It is possible that you have fallen prey to credit card fraud. Expenditures made without your consent or awareness. Identity theft can transpire when you employ your credit cards at establishments that lack security measures or when you provide your credit card details for an online transaction on unfamiliar platforms, resulting in the unauthorized acquisition of your sensitive financial information.

You possess an additional card user associated with your account, and there appears to have been a failure to coordinate respective expenditures, resulting in exceeding the prescribed limit on your card.

What constitutes credit card fraud?

As per the Businessdictionary.com definition, Credit Card Fraud refers to the deceptive utilization of a credit card account involving the illicit acquisition of the account holder's card number, detailed card information, and personal data, employing diverse methods, with the intention of executing unauthorized transactions from the compromised account. Credit card fraud is a legally prohibited offense and subject to legal consequences. It is imperative to refrain from engaging in legitimate purchases and subsequently falsely attributing them to credit card fraud.

Additional fundamental understanding of Credit Card Information (For Your Information)

Credit cards, similar to numerous other items, are commonly regarded as objects of social status.
- In the event of credit card loss or theft, one can promptly deactivate and obtain a replacement card by contacting the respective issuing financial institution.
Please refrain from recording your credit card number or lending your credit card to others.
The three-digit code located at the rear side of your credit card holds significant importance among the various codes associated with your card.
- It is highly advisable to commence educating young children concerning

financial matters at an early stage, particularly in terms of credit card debt.

"If you wish to discontinue your credit card, you have the option to settle the outstanding balance in full. Subsequently, you may compose a formal letter enclosing the card and explicitly instruct the bank to permanently deactivate it, e

Expression of Trust and Support (a universally desired sentiment)

If you find yourself burdened by credit card debt, it is possible to extricate yourself from this financial predicament. It is indeed challenging, but entirely feasible; it demands significant self-control and the willingness to forgo numerous desired acquisitions.

Closing Remarks

There exists an age-old adage that proclaims "slow and steady wins the race." This maxim applies to both savings and debt, as gradually adding "one one cocoa" will eventually lead to an empty basket.

Chapter 2

Could you please shed some light on the significance and value of effective monetary management?

Now, if one does not deem the management of one's financial resources significant or worthy of pursuit, it is highly unlikely that one will engage in such activities. Nevertheless, if you have perused this content thus far, I surmise that you attribute a certain degree of significance to the subject. I am unable to provide a comprehensive account of everyone's financial management experiences, but I can certainly share my own.
I was in my late adolescence and recently graduated from college, not yet having acquired my initial employment opportunity. Nonetheless, before long I was engaged in my tasks. In the past, my approach to money management was to

earn the income, settle the expenses, and utilize the remainder. This is a circumstance that I believe resonates with many individuals. However, it is important to acknowledge that there were instances in which I endeavored to save every penny, yet ultimately squandered all of it due to a sense of lacking in enjoyment and fulfillment. It constituted an exceedingly deleterious cycle that persisted for a span of several years until my engagement in a business venture precipitated my introduction to an entirely novel approach to fiscal management, unquestionably having a transformative impact on my life. Pretty much revolutionized it.

I currently possess excellent proficiency in financial management, a statement affirmed by my profound satisfaction derived from its benefits, namely the continuous growth of my wealth and assets. Currently, I am eagerly anticipating the acquisition and prudent handling of financial resources, as the prospect of monetary attainment fills me with enthusiasm.

Effective financial management provides individuals with the means to unlock personal autonomy and potentially serve as a source of inspiration. It enables you to attend to every facet of your existence without any sense of remorse. If one values autonomy, prosperity, realizing one's complete financial capabilities, and comprehensively embracing the opportunities that life presents, it is imperative to acquire the competence in effectively managing and stewarding one's financial resources.

Provided below are several compelling justifications illustrating the utmost significance of effectively managing one's financial resources.

- Encourages fiscal independence and prudent money management
-Aids in providing visibility to the allocation of your financial resources
-Financial growth
-Promotes wealth

-Encourages you to enhance your financial literacy

- Enhances the enjoyable factor when discussing the topic of money.

-Promotes the cultivation of relationships with individuals who possess sound financial knowledge and practices

- Facilitates liberty and safety - Provides opportunities for autonomy and protection - Supports individual rights and safeguards - Promotes personal liberties and ensures safety

- Your capacity to generate, retain, and expand your financial assets will be enhanced.

-Gives financial confidence

As you acquire proficiency in money management, it is inevitable that you will gradually recognize these aspects and experience personal growth concurrently. You will experience an increase in enthusiasm and excitement towards the topic, leading you to actively seek and discover methods to surpass your current financial situation.

Maintaining Financial Records

Surprisingly, a significant number of individuals are completely unaware of their current financial situation. They possess a profound lack of knowledge regarding the monetary value contained within their handbag or wallet, they lack any understanding of the funds held within their bank account, and they are completely unaware of the precise amount they expend utilizing their credit cards. It is imperative to maintain a record of your monetary resources in order to uphold your fiscal well-being.

personal welfare and tranquility of mind. It can be presumed that if you are aware of the exact amount of money you possess, you will acquire an immediate understanding regarding your ability to afford a purchase. Likewise, you will discern whether it is necessary to establish a financial plan."

for it first. You can rest assured that you won't have to worry about bounced checks, as well as being notified promptly about the accurate payment and management of your credit cards.

What a Bank Does

Are you aware of the process by which a financial institution generates profits? The most basic elucidation is that the bank generates revenue through the process of individuals depositing their funds with said bank, which in turn lends out those deposited funds to others (in exchange for a fee). The borrowers are then obligated to repay the loaned funds along with accruing interest. However, banks generate revenue through other means as well. In contemporary times, financial institutions incur numerous expenses, a considerable proportion of which may catch one off guard if not duly observed.

One financial institution may vary significantly from another in terms of the fees they impose. One financial institution will grant you free access to their automated teller machine (ATM) only if it is located at one of their branch locations; however, they will impose a fee if you opt to use an ATM situated in a grocery store. The cost of each transaction can amount to $1.50 or higher. An alternative financial institution will impose fees for every ATM transaction you make, each instance being subject to charges. One bank imposes a monthly fee of $6.95 for maintaining financial records, while another bank offers complimentary checking with the condition that the account holder writes no more than 20 checks.

or a monthly amount of fewer than. Typically, a single financial institution will offer multiple types of financial records, each accompanied by distinct services and associated fees. Attempt to gather comprehensive information about each variety so that you may select the most suitable option for your needs.

An alternative fee that incurs exorbitant costs and represents a significant waste of financial resources is the penalty for tardiness. If, by any chance, you happen to receive an advance and subsequently fail to make a timely payment, you might incur significantly substantial late fees, vastly exceeding your anticipated expectations. The banks favor the receipt of delayed expenditure funds. It represents a substantial portion of their income derived from individuals who fail to make timely payments.

Additionally, there are fees associated with bounce charges for checks. Creating a non-sufficient funds check refers to the act of issuing a check for a certain amount of cash despite the absence of sufficient funds in the associated bank account. Subsequently, the check is submitted to the bank for payment and subsequently returned to the issuer due to insufficient funds. Therefore, the banking institution imposes charges of $20.00 or more, even in instances where no funds are disbursed. The recipient or entity to whom you issued the check may also impose late fees or charges related to bounced checks, amounting to $20.00 or higher. It is unlikely that you will be the one responsible for drafting the check. You may be in possession of a friend's check, and it is possible that your friend's check may go uncashed. Notwithstanding the fact that it is not your concern, you may incur bank charges. You may consider distributing your money with little benefit while bearing the burden of these fees.

Depositing Checks

Upon commencing the establishment of financial records, one must first deposit cash into an account to issue checks. Subsequently, it becomes necessary to replenish the funds in the account by depositing both checks and currency. There are two pivotal pieces of information that you would want to handle in relation to your financial records and funds.

The initial factor to consider pertains to the method of endorsing a received check. To provide endorsement to a document, one must affix their signature on the reverse side. In the event that the rear of the check lacks a signature, it is incumbent upon the bank to refrain from depositing it into your account. Therefore, refrain from developing a tendency to cash a cheque immediately upon receiving it. In the event that the check is misplaced or confiscated, it is imperative to note that if it is not endorsed, it should not

Chapter 3: Keeping Track

possess the capacity to be employed by any individual. In the event that you indeed affix your signature, kindly be sure to include the designated record numbers, provided below, to prevent any possibility of it being erroneously deposited into a different account.

Therefore, you have securely retained possession of the check and now you are ready to endorse it and expeditiously deposit it into the bank or automated teller machine. What are the contents that you write on the rear side?

Please affix your endorsement on the designated area located at the reverse side of the document, typically indicated by the prompt 'Endorse Here.' Kindly note that you are provided with a limited space of approximately one inch for writing. The most effective course of action to ensure protection is to inscribe the phrase "For deposit only" together with your assigned checking (or savings account) number, followed by the affixing of your signature on the reverse side. If desired, it is possible to abbreviate the phrase "for deposit only" to "FDO." By including your account number on the check, you can ensure that the funds are credited into your account, safeguarding against the possibility of it being deposited into another individual's account. The endorsement is presented in the following manner:

The financial records in accordance with the C/A method. If we assume that S/A has been utilized, it will be designated for the purpose of depositing funds into a bank account.

The second pertinent piece of information you need to remember is that upon designating funds for check payment, those funds are not immediately available for your own expenditure. Numerous banks institute a mandatory waiting period during which they ensure the check is transferred from the issuing account and successfully deposited into your own account. Numerous individuals tend to issue checks on the same day they deposit or withdraw funds from their account, prior to the check being "cleared" or received by the bank.

The process of verifying funds by "clearing" the check from the issuing bank serves as confirmation that funds are available. Envision a hypothetical situation in which someone were to examine the check

wrote you bounces? Your bank would incur a financial loss as a result of transferring funds to another party, while not yet receiving the intended funds in return.

check you've deposited. As a result, you will incur penalties and be subject to check bouncing fees.

Frequently utilizing automated teller machines (ATMs) entails a longer processing time compared to visiting a bank teller, typically by approximately one day, as it involves the intermediary step of accessing funds from the banking institution. I understand that it may seem contradictory to think that using an electronic device capable of swiftly calculating monetary transactions would take more time than standing in front of a bank teller. However, the automated machines are operational and the paper checks are being processed.

The frequency of confirmation is diminishing with each passing day, consequently necessitating an additional day. It is strongly advisable to first save your money and subsequently make decisions regarding its use. Retain physical currency and allow for a grace period of approximately two business days prior to its expenditure. While certainly posing a considerable challenge, this will effectively spare you from incurring any overdraft fees on a recurring basis. It is advisable not to dismiss an amount ranging from $20.00 to $40.00.

Efforts to discover methods to guarantee the validity of the check you are issuing have been fruitless.

The sound of the chime does not reach the bank in an expeditious manner, thereby precluding any possibility of bouncing. There exists an alternative approach to expedite the process of receiving funds, whereby one would need to visit the bank of origin where the check was issued. In the circumstance where the check is issued from a Bank of America

To access your account, you may visit a Bank of America branch and deposit the check. This entails that you endorse the back of the check solely with your name, enabling the bank representative to provide you with cash in exchange.

Chapter 3: Keeping Track

The total indicated on the surface. A small number of banks may impose a fee if you do not hold an account with them.

Balance Your Checkbook

Ensuring that you do not expend your funds frivolously on unnecessary items prompts the need to diligently monitor the balance of available money in your account, which you have designated for expenditure. If you are unaware of the essential contents that should be maintained in your record consistently, various undesirable consequences could arise—most of them unfavorable for you but potentially advantageous for the bank.

Banking, even in the digital realm, is not immune to errors. Errors can occur both through the operation of machines and the actions of tellers. Errors may occur to your advantage or to the advantage of the financial institution. What course of action should be pursued if the bank levies an unjustifiable fee? Failure to reconcile your account on a regular basis would impede your ability to detect any potential financial discrepancies or missing funds. In the event that the financial institution mistakenly perceives insufficient funds in your account and declines a check issued by you, what would be the course of action? It is a costly error, yet it is remediable. You can

Recover your funds by promptly engaging in a discussion with the bank while ensuring that you possess supporting evidence.

Overall, how would you modify your documentation? For many individuals, this can be perplexing to some extent, even though it is actually a simple concept. The concept at hand is "What is the Bank's Knowledge?" and "What is Your Knowledge?" By diligently tracking all of your financial transactions, you will unfailingly possess more information than the bank. Subsequently, you need to ascertain the undisclosed information held by the bank, in order to ascertain your precise expendable funds.

Here's an example:

Your financial records currently reflect a balance of $400.00. On March 1st, a cheque in the amount of $600.00 was deposited. On March 4th, you issue a lease payment in the amount of $1000.00 to your designated property manager. Given that you attended your

If you were to visit the bank on March 4th and assess your bank balance, it would amount to $1000.00. This is the information that the bank would affirm is present in your records, as the bank does not possess prior knowledge of your circumstances.

composed a check. If you were to depend on that data and proceed to issue an additional check for food amounting to $45.00, and if both of these checks are presented for clearance in your bank on March 5, it is highly likely that one or both of these checks would be returned due to insufficient funds. Subsequently, you would incur considerable fees imposed by the bank for the resulting financial activity, as your account did not contain the necessary balance of $1045.00.

Individuals who neglect to prioritize their personal examination of transactions and instead rely solely on the opinion of the bank regarding their account balance are likely to frequently overlook checks and incur unnecessary banking fees. Banks provide customers with complimentary booklets, known as registers, specifically designed for meticulously documenting and reconciling all financial transactions. Presented herewith is an exemplary illustration of a contemporaneous check register:

With this knowledge at hand and the act of documenting it, you would possess the ability to ascertain

Prior to issuing Check #1045 in the amount of $45.00 for food, it would be necessary to deposit additional funds into the account, potentially requiring a one-day waiting period for its availability.

Effective financial management necessitates careful planning. Implementing proper arrangements can result in cost savings.

Incidentally, if you do indeed possess a financial account that imposes a monthly charge, it is advisable to never let your account balance reach zero, unless you also withdraw the corresponding fee for that particular month.

Chapter 3: Keeping Track

first. Assuming the bank deducts the $6.95 bank fee from your account, it will result in a negative balance. If you presume that the bank will notice the absence of funds in your account and opt to defer until further deposits are made, you will be greatly mistaken and it will incur financial expenses in the form of fees. You are likely understanding the concept at this juncture.

Is that what is referred to as 'modifying your documentation?' Not quite at that stage yet. The process of reconciling the record entails systematically comparing the bank's statement of transactions, which it believes to be accurate, with the confirm register to verify the bank's knowledge of these activities and identify any remaining tasks that still need to be addressed by the bank.

discover about.

Utilizing the aforementioned illustration, the bank statement for March 4 could appear as follows:

The bank possesses an excess of $1000.00 in closure funds. Your completion total amounts to $49.50. Adapting involves ensuring congruity between your figures and the banking figures. What method or approach would you employ to accomplish that?

1) Please mark all the bank transactions in your check register that correspond to one another. (Observe the region in the picture with the small indication of approval.)

2) Commencing with your closing balance of $49.50, augment it with any checks that you have issued subsequent to the bank statement transactions, subtract all deposits that have not yet been recorded by the bank, and you will arrive at your balance.

49.50

The representation would resemble this:

5.50

The total sum of $49.50, $5.50, $45.00, and $1000.00 equals $1100.00.

45.00 1000.00

$1100.00 minus 100.00 equals $1000.00, as per the bank's statement.

1100.00

finishing balance)

1100.00 That's it. You will correspond with the bank, aligning a sum of 100.00

in excess on one side with an equal amount on the other. 1000.00

What if we consider the possibility that the bank possesses a segment that you are not aware of, such as a monthly charge that you have overlooked? If the amount in question is indeed a legitimate debt owed to the bank, you will be required to subtract it from your final balance at the time of completion. The bank has deducted the amount and it is necessary for you to make a corresponding withdrawal as well. In the event of an error, you may promptly contact the bank to request their assistance in investigating the matter and facilitating the refund of your funds. If you persist in neglecting to reconcile your account, the banking institution will remain oblivious to the error, as will you, resulting in financial loss.

Is there any consideration regarding a previously issued check that remains undisclosed to the bank for a period of one month? Could you kindly disregard the matter and utilize the funds instead?

You are undoubtedly aware that the answer is "no."

According to the given model, supposing that you issued a lease payment check amounting to $1000.00 in February, it does not appear on the bank statement.

What are the key indicators of the economy?

The Gross Domestic Product (GDP) is commonly acknowledged by economists as the preeminent indicator of the present economic well-being of a nation. When the Gross Domestic Product (GDP) experiences growth, it serves as an indicator of a robust economic condition. An increase in GDP suggests economic growth, while a decrease implies contraction of the economy.

An ascending stock market generally reflects a expanding economy and engenders heightened investor assurance. Increased investor faith in stocks contributes to a heightened purchasing inclination, thereby facilitating upward price movement. When stock prices experience an increase, individuals with investments in the equity markets see a corresponding growth in their wealth.

Due to the fact that the stock market serves as an expression of confidence, a financial crash has the potential to significantly hinder economic expansion. Decreased stock prices result in diminished wealth for enterprises, pension funds, and individual investors. Enterprises may experience a shortfall in financing available for their operational and growth needs. A decline in the value of retirement funds leads to a curtailment in consumer expenditure, owing to the limited funds accessible for expenses.

Could you please provide some instances of both leading and lagging indicators?

Leading indicators afford you the chance to exert influence over forthcoming events, as they possess a forward-looking nature. The economy's key indicators of growth encompass manufacturing activity, the performance of the stock and housing markets, consumer sentiment, and the influx of new enterprises into the market.

Lagging indicators pertain to various economic metrics, for instance, gross domestic product (GDP), the consumer price index (CPI), and the balance of trade. These indicators exhibit variance from leading indicators, namely retail sales and the stock market, which are employed for the purposes of prognostication and forecast.

What indicators suggest the commencement of an economic recovery?

Unemployment continues to decrease.

There has been a continual rise in the creation of employment opportunities.

Emerging enterprises commence their establishment.

The resurgence of the Gross Domestic Product (GDP) commences.

Consumer and Producer Confidence are experiencing a notable upswing.

The housing market experiences a resurgence.

The equity market is experiencing a resurgence.

The Consumer Confidence Index (CCI) is widely regarded as a highly reliable gauge of consumer sentiments towards the economy and their individual circumstances. With the increase in employment opportunities, higher income levels, and reduction in interest rates, there is a subsequent boost in both consumer confidence and purchasing capacity. This phenomenon can significantly bolster stock prices.

What are the Indicators of a Looming Economic Recession?

An escalating unemployment rate often serves as a typical indicator of an imminent economic downturn.

Rising inflation.

Declining property sales.

The surging rate of delinquencies in credit card debt.

What is the time frame for the Markets to achieve a full recovery to their pre-crisis peak following a period of economic depression or recession?

It took approximately a quarter of a century for the financial markets to fully recuperate and return to their pre-crisis pinnacle following the significant decline experienced during the period of economic downturn known as the Great Depression in 1929. In contrast, it required approximately four years subsequent to the Great Recession of 2008-09 and an equivalent duration following the economic downturn of the 2000s.

Prominent instances of stock market crashes encompass the occurrences observed in the context of the Great Depression of 1929, the Black Monday event of 1987, the bursting of the dotcom bubble in 2001, the onset of the financial crisis in 2008, and the impact felt amid the COVID-19 pandemic in 2020.

What are the mechanisms through which Governments exert impact on Economic Growth?

A government has the ability to shape the pace of economic growth by implementing demand-side and supply-side policies. One such policy is expansionary fiscal measures, which involve reducing taxes to augment disposable income and stimulate expenditure. Nonetheless, a reduction in tax rates will elevate the budget deficit and result in heightened borrowing.

Economic growth holds significant importance as it serves as a crucial mechanism for enhancing the quality of our standard of living. Additionally, it empowers us to address any surges in our population without compromising our quality of life.

Economic stability serves as a foundational element for the attainment of various macroeconomic goals, including the maintenance of stable price levels and the facilitation of sustainable and consistent economic growth. Additionally, it fosters an ideal atmosphere for the generation of employment opportunities while also facilitating a favorable equilibrium within the balance of payments.

Increased savings can contribute to financing elevated levels of investment and enhancing productivity in the long run. In the field of economics, it is posited that the aggregate amount of savings corresponds to the aggregate amount of investment. Investment necessitates funding derived from savings. If individuals engage in higher levels of saving, it facilitates an increase in the amount of funds that banks can allocate towards lending to corporations for investment purposes.

What mechanisms does the South African Reserve Bank (SARB) employ to wield influence over Interest Rates and Inflation?

The South African Reserve Bank provides loans to commercial banks at the repurchase rate.

This facilitates the provision of liquidity to banks experiencing a deficit.

It entails a transitory transaction in which the bank temporarily vends a financial asset to the SARB, acquiring essential liquidity in return.

The bank intends to execute a repurchase agreement (repo) for the asset in question at a specified date in the future, such as within a week.

The determination of the repo rate is carried out by the South African Reserve Bank during its Monetary Policy Committee meeting.

The repo rate functions as a reference point for determining short-term interest rates.

Through the repo rate, the SARB indirectly has a strong influence on all the short term interest rates in the banking system.

If inflation exceeds the government's set inflation target of 3-6%, it imposes constraints on the inflationary trajectory as follows:

SARB raises repo rate.

Financial institutions are obliged to raise their lending and deposit rates in order to uphold their profit margins.

This measure effectively mitigates inflationary pressures by curbing the need for credit to finance the acquisition of goods and services. The consumer's inclination towards making credit purchases has decreased

This effectively inhibits the escalation of prices and wages.

Inflation is reduced.

When inflation levels dip below the prescribed inflation target range, the South African Reserve Bank (SARB) proceeds to lower the repo rate, triggering a subsequent series of actions in the opposite direction. In order to curb excessive credit growth and money supply expansion, lending rates should be set at a level significantly above the inflation rate.

Food for thought:
Economics holds a paramount significance in our day-to-day existence. It exerts an influence on our lives,

encompassing both a broader societal level and an individual level. Elements such as prevailing interest rates, inflation levels, fluctuations in economic growth and stability, unemployment rates, and the overall gross domestic product exert an impact on the lives of individuals every day. These variables ascertain the caliber of our lives and the day-to-day choices we undertake in regards to long-term investments. Furthermore, a strong correlation exists between the economy and the stock market, wherein each exerts a direct influence on the other.